CW01082905

Original title:
I Hope This Helps

Editor: Theodor Taimla
Author: Lisanne Liustik
ISBN HARDBACK: 978-9916-756-66-9
ISBN PAPERBACK: 978-9916-756-67-6

Small Sparks

In the quiet, a whisper calls,
Through the night, a flame ignites.
Dreams awaken within these walls,
Guiding hearts through starry nights.

Beneath the clamor, gentle gleam,
Voices soft, yet thunder strong.
Each small spark, a vivid dream,
Lighting paths our souls belong.

In the hush, a spark will rise,
Bold and bright, unfurl its wings.
With each dawn, a new surprise,
Hidden hope in simple things.

Anchors in the Storm

When the winds begin to howl,
And the waves crash with disdain.
Find your anchor, strong and foul,
Steer your ship through roaring rain.

In the tempest, steadfast heart,
Hold your course when skies grow dark.
Steady hands will do their part,
Guiding through each lightning spark.

Through the storm, the anchor stays,
Rooted firm beneath the blast.
Calm will follow, sunlit rays,
Stronger bonds from trials past.

Notes of Encouragement

A gentle word, a knowing smile,
Can lift a soul from darkest plight.
Through the weary, longest mile,
Bring the dawn from endless night.

Every note of love we give,
Sends a ripple far and wide.
Helping others learn to live,
Strength through kindness multiplied.

In each step, and every voice,
Echoes hope through storm and calm.
In the sharing, we rejoice,
Hearts and spirits, soothed like balm.

Embracing Change

New horizons call our name,
Whispers of the vast unknown.
In the shift, we bloom and flame,
Changing paths where seeds are sown.

Fear not what the future brings,
For in change, the soul will grow.
In the breeze of newfound wings,
Find your strength in ebb and flow.

Embrace the change, let seasons wend,
In each turn, a lesson worn.
Through the labyrinth, hearts commend,
New beginnings yet unborn.

A Drink from the Well

In the heart of fields, it stands tall,
A silent witness to the call.
Spilling whispers, deep, profound,
A timeless echo in the ground.

Clear as crystal, pure as night,
Reflecting stars in gentle light.
Drawing life from ages past,
To quench the thirst that ever lasts.

Beneath the boughs, where shadows play,
Children laugh and old men pray.
A sacred font for every soul,
Filling hearts to make them whole.

Steps of Serenity

Along the trail where quiet leads,
Through whispering grass and swaying reeds.
A path unfolds in nature's grace,
Blessed with calm and endless space.

Footfalls gentle, almost air,
Breathing in the tranquil fare.
Each step echoes, soft and light,
Guided by day, cradled by night.

Here the heart finds its repair,
In steps that mend, in breaths that care.
May every soul be lightly steered,
To serenity's door, dearly revered.

Bridging the Gap

Between the hills, a span of dreams,
Crossing over murmuring streams.
Connecting lands and hearts alike,
A beacon through the mist and pike.

Stone by stone, the arch was born,
A compass through the thickest thorn.
Bridging gaps where none could see,
Forging bonds eternally.

Step upon this path of hope,
Where shadows cease and spirits cope.
United by a common tread,
Towards the future, boldly led.

Finding Footing

In the dance of life, feet find their place,
Moving in rhythm, a tender grace.
Step by step, through joy and strife,
Carving the pathway, embracing life.

Roots hold firm in shifting sands,
Grasping tightly to hesitant hands.
Steady now, in moments bright,
Honing courage with each flight.

Bound by faith, the journey's start,
To find the footing of the heart.
With every stumble, rise anew,
Finding strength in all you do.

Safe Harbor Found

Waves crash against the steadfast shore,
As the sun sets, casting golden light.
In this haven of peace, worries no more,
A sailor's heart finds calm tonight.

Anchored dreams in twilight's embrace,
Gentle winds whisper lullabies true.
Stars like guides in the vast space,
Promise dawn with skies clear and blue.

Safe within this harbor's gentle arms,
Where the tempest's fury fades away.
Love and hope as trustworthy charms,
Guard us from the storm's harsh sway.

Mending Gently

In quiet moments, hearts repair,
With threads of kindness, tender care.
Soft-spoken words, a soothing hand,
Rebuild the bridges where we stand.

Gentle as the morning mist,
Healing comes in every kiss.
From broken pieces, a mosaic grand,
Mending gently, we understand.

In the cocoon of night's embrace,
We gather strength to face the race.
With every dawn, a promise new,
To mend our hearts and spirits too.

Buoy in Rough Seas

Amidst the torrent, steadfast bright,
A beacon in the darkest night.
Guiding sailors through the storm,
Where waves and winds with fury swarm.

Buoy resilient, never swayed,
In chaos, its light displayed.
A symbol of hope, a promise kept,
So all may find where peace is swept.

In raging seas where tempests howl,
Unyielding, standing firm and proud.
Buoys in rough seas, life's guiding light,
Assure safe passage through the fight.

Tender Voice

In whispers soft that melt the night,
A tender voice can bring the light.
Its gentle tones a healing balm,
In stormy hearts, restoring calm.

Words laced with love, like morning dew,
Reviving spirits, fresh and new.
A voice that soothes the deepest woe,
And helps the fragile heart to grow.

In every sound, a touch so kind,
A melody to ease the mind.
Through tender voice, we find our way,
To brighter nights and peaceful day.

Echoes of Empathy

Within the silent chambers, hearts do blend,
A whisper shared where souls intend,
Tiny sparks of kindness, softly roam,
In empathy's embrace, we've found our home.

In the wake of tears, we stand as one,
Woven threads where hearts are spun,
The gentle touch, an unseen hand,
Echoes of love across the land.

Understanding eyes reflect the pain,
With each other's strength, we mend again,
No need for words, the silence speaks,
Together in empathy, solace we seek.

Hopeful Horizons

Beyond the twilight's velvet guise,
Hope awakens, dreams arise,
Golden hues of dawn break free,
Horizons call, invitingly.

Through darkest nights and tempest's rage,
Hope's a light upon the stage,
Guiding hearts with gentle beams,
Toward horizons, laced with dreams.

Whispers of tomorrow sing,
In the heart where hope takes wing,
A promise painted in the sky,
Hopeful horizons, ever nigh.

Comfort in Chaos

In the whirlwind of life's race,
Amidst the chaos, find your place,
A stillness born from inner peace,
Comfort's touch, a sweet release.

Through the storm, resilience shows,
In the strife, our spirit grows,
A tranquil heart, a calming voice,
In chaos, find the quiet choice.

Amid the noise, a soothing sound,
Harmony in turmoil found,
A tender hand, a gentle guide,
Comfort within chaos doth reside.

Soft Echoes

In quiet halls, soft echoes sing,
Whispers of forgotten spring,
Memories in gentle flow,
Soft as dreams we used to know.

Words unspoken, yet they stay,
Lingering in twilight's gray,
Embers of the past remain,
In soft echoes, love's refrain.

Through the years, these echoes drift,
A tender touch, a fleeting gift,
Soft reminders, ever near,
Echoes of a time so dear.

Infinite Impact

In a world vast and grand,
Ripple effects start from a hand,
Small deeds expand like the sea,
Binding us in unity.

Whispers of hope softly tell,
Of changes where kind acts dwell,
A smile, a word, or a glance,
Gives life's purpose, a chance.

As stars are born in the night,
From small sparks ignites light,
Through actions both brave and small,
We touch the hearts of all.

Though the waves may seem slight,
They turn darkness into light,
In each gesture, we find,
The power of humankind.

Infinite echoes resound,
In a circle so profound,
From one to another we move,
With love, our paths improve.

Veil of Kindness

In the silence of the morn,
A gentle veil is worn,
Covering hearts with grace,
In every quiet place.

Tender hands softly weave,
Threads of what we believe,
Kindness shrouds the soul bright,
Guiding us in the night.

Whispered words, kind and true,
Heal the old and the new,
Under veils, we find peace,
Where compassion will not cease.

As the veil descends light,
It warms the coldest night,
In its folds, we see,
The world as it could be.

Through the veil, we can reach,
Hearts with lessons to teach,
One act, from you and me,
Unveils humanity.

Ladders of Hope

In shadows deep, we start to climb,
With every step, a brighter chime.
Grasping firm, our dreams align,
To visions where the stars entwine.

Though fears may rise like tides anew,
Our hearts ignite, with courage true.
Each rung we conquer, skies so blue,
Awakes within, horizons view.

Hand in hand, through storm and gale,
Together strong, we'll never fail.
Hope ascends, a silver rail,
On ladders woven, endless trail.

Burden Lessened

The weight we carry, day by day,
Can lighten with a gentle sway.
A shared smile, we'll find a way,
To turn the night to dawn's soft ray.

In whispers of a friend so dear,
Our troubles seem to disappear.
With every step, they'll hold us near,
And burdens lessened, calm and clear.

A kindred spirit by our side,
Together strong, with love as guide.
Through storm or peace, hearts open wide,
Our worries drift, like ebbing tide.

Candles in the Night

In darkest hours, they softly glow,
A flicker guides the path below.
Candles in the night bestow,
A light that helps the spirit grow.

Through shadows thick, their light persists,
In quiet whispers, hope insists.
A warmth that every soul assists,
In night's embrace, a gentle kiss.

By these flames, we find our way,
A dance of light keeps fear at bay.
Through every trial, oceans gray,
Candles in the night will stay.

Embers of Encouragement

In the hearth of human heart,
Embers glow as dreams restart.
Gentle whispers form an art,
Encouragement, a healing chart.

Each spark ignites a field of grace,
Lighting up the darkest space.
Hand in hand, we find our place,
In embers, we see love's embrace.

As ashes fade and dawn renew,
These embers carry courage through.
In every heart, they softly grew,
Inspiration's touch, forever true.

Wind beneath Wings

A whisper through the leaves, it sings
Silent promise to the sky
On gentle gales, our hearts take flight
To dreams that never die

Emerald seas in endless dance
With songs of old and new
A canvas of the heavens' chance
Our spirits to renew

Feathered grace in azure light
Rising, free to soar
The breeze that lifts, beyond our sight
Unlocks a boundless door

With every ebb, a story spun
Of worlds where freedom rings
Through twilight's veil and morning's sun
The wind beneath our wings

Nurtured by Night

In the hush of twilight's fold
Stars unveil the calm'd night sea
With silver whispers, stories told
Of dreams that come to be

Luna's grace, a tender sway
Comfort in her gentle gleam
Beneath her watch, our fears allay
And hearts begin to dream

Shadows dance in silent grace
Their secrets softly spun
In night's embrace, we find our place
'Til rise of morning sun

Cradle of the silent hours
In darkness, strength we find
Nurtured by night's quiet flowers
To leave our doubts behind

Sunlight on Shadows

Golden threads in morning light
Chase shadows from the night
With each new dawn, a promise bright
Hope's flame is reignited

Where darkness clings, soft beams emerge
A silent, gentle plea
To heal and warm, to softly urge
Our hearts from sorrow free

In every shadow cast by sun
A lesson time bestows
That light can heal where night has spun
And beauty ever grows

Sunlight dances, whispers clear
Over every hidden face
In shadows deep, we see and hear
The dawn's redeeming grace

Mosaic of Mercy

In fragments time has gently placed
A mosaic, pure and kind
With every shard of broken grace
A masterpiece we find

From pain and joy, from loss and love
This tapestry we weave
A work of art from high above
In which our souls believe

Mercy's hand in tender care
Shapes us through life's storm
A thousand colors, bold and fair
A portrait to transform

In every piece, a story held
Of lessons we once knew
A mosaic where our hearts are spelled
In shades of mercy's hue

Healing Threads

In silent whispers, the fabric mends,
Threads of hope through sorrow blend.
Wounds may scar but softly heal,
Love's tender stitch, the pain will steal.

From frayed beginnings, strength is spun,
In every heart, a thread begun.
Hands that weave through darkest night,
Crafting dawns of purest light.

With each new morning, colors bloom,
Pains dissolve, making room.
In woven tales, we find our way,
Healing threads, a brighter day.

White Light of Love

A white light shines, pure and near,
Guiding hearts through every fear.
In the glow, we find our place,
Love's embrace, a warm embrace.

From shadows deep, a beacon bright,
Shattering the darkest night.
With every touch and whispered word,
Love's gentle power, softly heard.

Within its glow, new dreams ignite,
A symphony of radiant light.
Through trials long and journeys wide,
White light of love, our constant guide.

Sparks of Encouragement

In quiet moments, whispers rise,
A spark of hope beneath the skies.
Encouragement, like stars above,
Lights the path with endless love.

Through valleys deep and mountains high,
A gentle word can lift us high.
In every heart, a fire ignites,
Sparks of courage, burning bright.

With every step, a new refrain,
Shared words to heal and ease the pain.
In unity, we find our strength,
Encouragement, a light's great length.

Rest for the Weary

Upon the shores of quiet dreams,
A place of peace from life's extremes.
Soft whispers call the weary home,
To fields where troubles cease to roam.

Under skies of twilight blue,
Rest awaits for me, for you.
In gentle hands, our burdens fall,
A tranquil night, a restful call.

With every breath, a calm descends,
A soothing balm that gently mends.
Within this haven, hearts find peace,
In rest for weary, woes release.

Silent Blessings

In the hush of dawn, the whispers come,
Soft and gentle, like a distant drum.
Glimmers of hope in a muted song,
Blessings silent, yet ever so strong.

The world awakens with a tender grace,
Echoes of kindness fill the space.
Silent moments, quietly profound,
In hidden blessings, beauty is found.

A fleeting glance, a touch unseen,
In the quiet, our hearts convene.
Gentle whispers in the morning light,
Blessings silent, hold us tight.

The day marches on, with silent cheer,
Blessings hidden, ever near.
In moments hushed, our souls can rest,
Silent blessings, we are blessed.

Under the stars, as night descends,
With silent blessings, our hearts mend.
Restful sleep in the moon's embrace,
Silent blessings, a sacred space.

Hidden Strengths

Beneath the surface, deep inside,
Strengths unknown begin to bide.
In quiet resolve, they slowly grow,
Hidden strengths we come to know.

The storm may rage, the winds may blow,
But inner strength continues to flow.
In moments tough, it shows its might,
Hidden strengths take flight in the night.

Through trials faced and challenges met,
Hidden strengths we won't forget.
In every stumble, in each fall,
We find our hidden strengths, standing tall.

In whispered fears, in silent cries,
Strengths emerge, to our surprise.
A reservoir we never knew,
Hidden strengths come shining through.

When doubt and fear cloud our way,
Hidden strengths light the day.
In darkest times, they lead us on,
Through hidden strengths, battles are won.

Odes to Optimism

In the light of dawn, a new day gleams,
Optimism flows like sunlit streams.
Beneath the clouds, the sun will rise,
With hope anew, we greet the skies.

Every challenge is a chance to grow,
Optimism sets our hearts aglow.
With each step forward, we embrace,
The endless possibilities we chase.

In shadows deep, a light persists,
Optimism's song, it softly insists.
Through doubts and fears, it finds its way,
To brighter thoughts, it leads the day.

In every tear, a lesson lies,
Optimism helps the spirit rise.
With dreams unbound, we take our flight,
Odes to optimism, our guiding light.

Through winding roads and paths unknown,
Optimism makes us feel at home.
In every heart, its fire burns,
Odes to optimism, the world turns.

Gentle Guidance

With hands so light and voice so clear,
Gentle guidance draws us near.
In paths uncertain, in times of doubt,
Gentle words lead us out.

A calm embrace, a soothing tone,
In gentle guidance, we aren't alone.
Through storms of life, through trials untold,
Gentle guidance, strong and bold.

With every step, with each breath,
Gentle guidance wards off death.
A steady hand to show the way,
In gentle guidance, fears decay.

Through darkest nights, when hope seems thin,
Gentle guidance whispers within.
It lights a path, it shows the truth,
In gentle guidance, lies our youth.

In moments fraught, in fleeting peace,
Gentle guidance brings release.
With heart and soul, it calls us home,
Gentle guidance, never alone.

Voices of Empathy

In echoes soft, we hear the pleas,
Of hearts that yearn, of silent seas.
With tender thoughts, we bridge the gaps,
In empathy, the globe perhaps.

A whisper shared, a gentle nod,
Compassion's light, a shared applaud.
To stand with grace, to feel their plight,
In voices calm, we find our sight.

For every tear, a willing ear,
Transforming pain to hope sincere.
In kindness pure, we intertwine,
In empathy, our spirits shine.

Through storms unknown, through darkest night,
We light the way, we share our light.
For in each heart, a story lives,
And empathy, our story gives.

We walk as one, through fire and rain,
In unison, through joy and pain.
In voices soft, we understand,
For empathy, we lend a hand.

Found in Friendship

In moments shared, in laughter bright,
Friendship blooms in morning light.
A bond so true, so deep and clear,
In every joy, in every tear.

Through winding roads, through paths unknown,
A friend is there, you're not alone.
With hands to hold and hearts to cheer,
In friendship strong, we persevere.

With whispered dreams and secret tales,
A friendship's strength, it never pales.
In darkest nights, in brightest days,
In friendship's warmth, forever stays.

Through ups and downs, through thick and thin,
A friend is where we both begin.
In trust we find a strength anew,
In friendship, we remain true.

And though the years may pass and fade,
The memories we've surely made,
Will stand the test, will always last,
In friendship's light, we're anchored fast.

Strength in Solidarity

From hands that clasp in unity,
A strength is born, a bond set free.
In solidarity's embrace,
We find our power, our common space.

When voices rise in one accord,
We shift the world, we wield the sword.
In unity, we stand so strong,
In righting every ancient wrong.

With hearts aligned, with shared resolve,
Together, we will not dissolve.
In times of need, in moments dire,
Solidarity's eternal fire.

For justice calls and we respond,
In solidarity, beyond.
With courage fierce, we face the night,
In unity, we find the light.

Through every storm, through darkest seas,
We hold the line, we bend the knees.
In strength found in our unity,
Solidarity sets us free.

Ripples of Relief

In gentle waves of calm and peace,
We cast away, we find release.
With every whisper, every sigh,
Relief is found, soars sky-high.

In solace brief, in quiet thought,
Relief's embrace, serenely caught.
We breathe anew, we find our way,
Through ripples cast by light of day.

The weight is lifted, burdens eased,
In simple acts, in hearts appeased.
With gentle hands, with calming care,
Relief is found, it's everywhere.

Through tides of time, through ebb and flow,
Relief's embrace, we come to know.
In moments small, in grander schemes,
Relief is found in woven dreams.

With open hearts, with softened eyes,
We see the world in clearer skies.
In every act of shared belief,
We cast anew ripples of relief.

Heartfelt Steadiness

In the quiet dawn of day
With whispers soft and tender
Your steadfast heart, a calming bay
Guides me through storms to render

When shadows creep and thunder roars
Your presence stands unbroken
A lighthouse on love's distant shores
With words of strength unspoken

In every step, your heartbeat's grace
A rhythm pure and steady
You lift me to a higher place
Where dreams and hope are ready

Our journey's path may twist and weave
Through valleys dark and dreary
Yet in your love, I do believe
And find my solace clearly

Heartfelt steadiness, love's pure ground
Your essence ever guiding
In you, a sanctuary found
In trust and love abiding

Lighthouse of Kindness

Through night's embrace, your light does gleam
A beacon bright and true
Your kindness flows, a gentle stream
To guide and see me through

When tempests rise and hopes are frayed
Your grace remains unyielding
A lighthouse where my soul is swayed
In warmth and comfort, shielding

Compassion's glow within you burns
A flame that never wanes
In every heart your care returns
To heal life's weary strains

Forgiveness softens every blow
Your kindness never falters
In darkest depths, a steady glow
True path that never alters

Lighthouse of kindness, pure and bright
Your beacon calls to me
In you, I find my guiding light
And set my spirit free

Trust in the Tide

As evening falls on weary seas
We trust the tide will turn
With every wave, in gentle ease
Our hearts begin to learn

Endless ebb and gentle flow
A cycle born of time
In trust, we let our worries go
The waves, a soothing rhyme

On endless shores, we place our feet
Where tides caress the sand
In faith, the ocean's heart we meet
And trust the unseen hand

Through tempests wild and calmest night
The tide is always true
In darkest depths or morning light
Its strength we will renew

So trust in the tide, the sea's embrace
Let currents lead the way
In every wave, we find our place
Through night and into day

Cradle of Compassion

In gentle arms of compassion's hold
Our bruised hearts find repair
A cradle wrought of love pure gold
A refuge from despair

Where tears fall free and sorrow's felt
Your kindness wraps around
In womb of empathy, we melt
A sanctuary found

Through trials faced and heavy loads
Your heart remains as shelter
In darkened times, compassion flows
A soft embrace, a welter

In deepest depths of human pain
Your love becomes our guide
A beacon through the harshest rain
In you, our fears subside

Cradle of compassion, ever bold
In you, our solace lies
With tender touch, our hearts you hold
Beneath life's stormy skies

From Worry to Wonder

In shadows deep our worries lie,
But dawn reveals a brighter sky.
Each star that fades away in night,
Returns as dreams within our sight.

With every breath, a chance to pause,
To shed our fears, embrace what was.
For in our hearts a brighter spark,
Turns doubt to light against the dark.

The burdens heavy on our soul,
Like autumn leaves will softly roll.
Transforming all that held us tight,
To gentle winds and skies alight.

So let us wander, free from care,
To find the magic in the air.
For every worry cast aside,
Opens our hearts, a wondrous tide.

Fountains of Faith

From ancient wells where hope springs clear,
Flows faith that whispers in our ear.
In gentle streams of pure belief,
It washes clean our deepest grief.

The currents strong and always near,
Through trials faced, we persevere.
In every drop, a sign to see,
That love and trust will set us free.

Where doubts dissolve like morning mist,
Our spirits rise, by faith we're kissed.
For every hardship fades away,
In holy light, our fears allay.

So drink from fountains wide and deep,
In faith, our souls shall always keep.
A bond unbroken, strong as stone,
Guiding us back to hope's bright home.

Gardens of Grace

In meadows where the wildflowers grow,
A garden blooms with gentle glow.
Each petal whispers soft embrace,
In nature's touch, we find our place.

With every season's tender care,
The earth provides beyond compare.
For in these gardens pure and free,
Lies boundless grace for you and me.

The morning dew like silver threads,
Adorns the grass where beauty spreads.
And in the quiet hum of bees,
We hear the song of endless ease.

So let us tend with gracious hands,
These sacred plots of blessed lands.
For in each bloom, a symbol true,
Of grace that lives in all we do.

Spreading Solace

When hearts are heavy with the night,
And all our hopes seem out of sight.
A gentle word, a kind embrace,
Brings solace in the darkest place.

In whispers soft or acts so small,
Kindness rises to break our fall.
Through tender care, our spirits mend,
In every smile, a faithful friend.

The light of solace spreads around,
In every corner, peace is found.
With every touch, a wound can heal,
And love's true power we reveal.

So let us scatter seeds of grace,
To brighten every lonely space.
For in this world, a single heart,
Can spread the solace, play its part.

Unseen Heroes

In quiet shadows, they remain
With strength of heart, they bear the strain
The silent knights of everyday
In unseen ways, they find their way

Unsung, unpraised, yet always there
With tender hands and gentle care
In smallest acts, they light the night
Their humble hearts, our guiding light

In bustling streets and humble homes
Through every trial, their spirit roams
Anonymous, they stand their ground
In whispers, their great deeds are found

For every tear, a comfort near
In unseen acts, they quell the fear
They walk with grace, unknown, unsung
In hidden ways, their praise is sung

With quiet might, they shape the day
Unseen heroes, who light our way

Resilient Reflections

In mirrors deep, a soul reflects
Through trials faced, with no regrets
The scars of time, they mark the face
Yet inner light does not erase

Resilience born from endless flight
In darkest hours, finding light
With heavy hearts, still moving on
The dawn awaits, a newer dawn

In whispers of the midnight air
A strength that grows, beyond despair
Through tears that fall like gentle rain
Emerges grace from deepest pain

For every shadow, there's a star
Each wound a story, near and far
In broken chains, they find their wings
With steadfast hearts, the hopeful sing

Resilient souls, they rise again
In heartache, finding strength within
Through every storm, they stand tall
Reflections of a spirit strong for all

Pathways of Peace

Upon a path of quiet stone
The whispers of the world unknown
In every step, a breath released
Through tranquil walks, a soul's at peace

Among the trees, a gentle song
The world in harmony prolongs
A silent stream of thoughts unspoken
In nature's arms, the heart is open

Through winding trails, the spirit soars
In peaceful strides, the heart restores
With every breath, the burdens fade
On pathways where no shadows wade

In quiet glades, the mind finds rest
A sanctuary, nature's crest
In stillness, finding all that's lost
The peace of mind, beyond all cost

Through pathways carved in earth and sky
A journey where the spirits fly
In peace, they find their simple grace
With every step, a new embrace

From Fear to Faith

In darkest hours, fear takes hold
With trembling hearts and voices cold
Yet through the darkness, light appears
The dawn of faith, it dries the tears

From shadows deep, a spark ignites
In every heart, a war it fights
To banish fear, replace with trust
In faith, the heart can rise, it must

With every doubt, a chance to grow
Through trials faced, the truth we know
That faith is born from fear's embrace
A journey toward a safer place

With every step, the fear subsides
In faith, a stronger heart abides
Through stormy seas, the ship holds fast
In faith, our anchor strong and vast

From fear to faith, a path we tread
With courage born from tears we've shed
In faith, we find our way to light
From darkest night to morning bright

Trust in Tomorrow

The world spins on, both day and night,
In shadows deep, in morning's light,
Through darkest hours, the dawn breaks free,
A new day holds our destiny.

On paths unknown, our hearts remain,
With dreams of joy, and hope from pain,
Each step we take, towards the new,
For tomorrows bright, for skies of blue.

Though storms may come, and tears may flow,
In every heart, the seeds we sow,
Will bloom with time, with love and care,
And guide us onward, everywhere.

When doubts arise, and fears encroach,
Trust in the future's soft approach,
For even in the bleakest night,
The morning sun brings forth its light.

So lift your gaze, and walk with pride,
With faith as strong, as oceans wide,
For every end, a start awaits,
In life's grand dance, through Heaven's gates.

Silent Support

In quiet ways, they stand beside,
No words exchanged, no tears to hide,
A presence felt, in every breath,
Their love a shield, against life's death.

When burdens weigh, and hearts are sore,
In silence, they give something more,
A touch, a glance, a warmth to share,
Their silent support, forever there.

Through tempests wild, and through despair,
In shadows deep, they show their care,
No need for praise, no call to fame,
Their strength, a light without a name.

In every step, in each small gain,
Their silent hope, becomes our lane,
A path to peace, through trials vast,
Their love, an anchor, to hold fast.

So cherish those who stay unseen,
In love, through quiet ways they mean,
More than the loudest, proudest cheer,
Their silent support, is crystal clear.

Guiding Stars

In nights so dark, where shadows play,
The stars above, will light the way,
A guiding hand, from realms afar,
Our dreams, they capture in a jar.

Through depths of space, their light does gleam,
Fulfilling hope in every dream,
No path too long, no night too vast,
Their glow a beacon, sure to last.

As wanderers seek truth and aim,
The stars align, they bear no shame,
With whispers soft, they call our names,
And lead us through life's varied games.

In choices made, in paths we choose,
Their guiding light, we never lose,
Hold firm your gaze, when all seems lost,
For stars guide true, at any cost.

So look above, let worries fade,
In starry light, our hopes remade,
With trust in stars, both near and far,
We find our way, no matter where we are.

A Hand to Hold

In times of need, in moments cold,
There waits for us, a hand to hold,
A simple touch, a grasp so warm,
To shield us from, life's raging storm.

When fears arise, and courage wanes,
A hand will pull us from our pains,
Through darkest days, through trials wide,
In clasped hands, we find our guide.

No words required, no grand display,
A hand held tight, will light the way,
Connections deep, through touch conveyed,
In unity, our fears allayed.

For every soul, a match is made,
A hand to hold, through light and shade,
In ups and downs, in joy and plight,
Together strong, we'll face the night.

So reach out close, and hold on tight,
In hands entwined, we gain our might,
For love and strength, in hands unfold,
In life's great journey, a hand to hold.

Calm Amidst the Waves

Beneath the sky's vast, endless dome,
Where currents swirl like ocean foam,
A calmness dwells within the heart,
Serenity, a tranquil art.

Though tempests rise and thunder roars,
And waves crash wild upon the shores,
In quiet moments, peace will find,
A haven calm, within the mind.

Amidst the storm, a stillness lies,
A silent strength, beneath the skies.
With every wave, a lesson learned,
In calm, life's chaos overturned.

Threads of Kindness

In the tapestry of time unwound,
Where every thread of life is found,
Kindness weaves its gentle hue,
A pattern soft, yet ever true.

With every act, a thread is spun,
A gift of light for everyone.
In moments shared, connections grow,
A weave of love, a gentle flow.

When darkness falls and hope is thin,
Kindness lights a spark within.
A tapestry, both vast and kind,
Threads of love, in hearts entwined.

Whispers of Comfort

In shadows cold, where silence reigns,
A whisper soft, like gentle rains.
Comfort comes in tender sighs,
A breath of peace, to soothe our cries.

When sorrow's weight is hard to bear,
And life feels lost in deep despair,
A whisper speaks, a quiet grace,
A touch of comfort, warm embrace.

Through darkest nights, and endless days,
In whispered love, the heart conveys.
A solace found in softest tone,
Whispers of comfort, not alone.

Whispers in the Wind

The wind it blows a gentle kiss,
Through trees it murmurs secrets true,
In gales and gusts, an ancient bliss,
A touch of sky in every hue.

Leaves they dance, a ballet grand,
A symphony of rustling sound,
Nature's orchestra, unplanned,
In whispers, magic can be found.

Clouds drift by like ships at sea,
Sailing skies, so vast and blue,
Wind's soft song, a melody,
An endless hymn for me and you.

Mountains echo every breeze,
Their silent strength a guiding hand,
In whispers, nature grants us ease,
A language only hearts understand.

The wind it holds a timeless grace,
A fleeting caress, cool and kind,
In its whispers we find our place,
A gentle guide, a soothing mind.

A Friendly Nudge

A smile can change the world we see,
A beacon in the darkest night,
A friendly nudge can set us free,
It turns the gloom to pure delight.

A hand to hold in times of strife,
A promise that we're not alone,
Such gestures brighten up our life,
A love that goes forever shown.

A word of kindness, softly said,
Can lift the heaviest of hearts,
In friendly nudges we are led,
To where true joy and peace start.

Compassion's touch, a gentle guide,
A whisper of the soul's embrace,
In friendship's warmth we can confide,
And find a safe and sacred space.

A friendly nudge, a simple gift,
Yet powerful in all it brings,
It carries us, it helps us lift,
To find the strength within our wings.

Lifting Spirits

When shadows fall and light seems dim,
A gentle word can brighten skies,
In kindness, hope begins to brim,
A spark within each heart to rise.

A laugh, a cheer, a helping hand,
In trying times, we find our strength,
Together, we do understand,
The joy that goes to any length.

In every smile, a world anew,
In every hug, a soothing balm,
When spirits lift, the skies turn blue,
A realm of peace, a calming calm.

With open hearts and minds we soar,
Above the clouds, our dreams take flight,
In unity, we find much more,
A shared embrace of endless light.

So let us lift each spirit high,
With love, with hope, and gentle care,
Together, we can touch the sky,
In endless joy, our burdens share.

Moments to Mend

In silence we may find the ways,
To heal the wounds we cannot see,
In quiet, thoughtful, tender days,
We mend, we grow, we set hearts free.

A pause to breathe, a time to hold,
The fragments of a weary soul,
In moments calm, our tales unfold,
And broken pieces start to whole.

Through gentle words and softest touch,
We learn to mend what once was torn,
In simple acts that mean so much,
A healing path is freshly born.

Moments to mend, they come like rain,
To cleanse the past and wash our fears,
In every drop, a sweet refrain,
That soothes our troubles, dries our tears.

With time and care, the heart repairs,
In love's embrace, we start again,
Through tender moments, gentle prayers,
We find the strength to mend, to reign.

Seeds of Change

In earth so firm, we plant our dream,
Through sun and rain, a constant theme,
With tender care, in soil they lie,
To reach for stars, to touch the sky.

From tiny seeds, great oaks arise,
Through storms and calms, beneath the skies,
Their roots dig deep, their branches sway,
A testament to each new day.

With every bloom, we learn and grow,
Embracing winds, both high and low,
The past a whisper, futures vast,
In gardens green, time moves fast.

The gardener's hand, both swift and kind,
Nurtures life, the threads that bind,
For in each shoot, a promise made,
Of hope renewed, of fears allayed.

Lifted by Love

In tender arms, a warm embrace,
A love so pure, a sacred space,
Through joy and sorrow, hand in hand,
Together strong, we firmly stand.

With every beat, our hearts align,
A bond so deep, a love divine,
Through darkest nights, in lightning's glare,
We find our strength in moments rare.

The whispering breeze, the songs we share,
Memories made, beyond compare,
In fleeting time, our spirits rise,
Lifted by love, beyond the skies.

No fear remains, when love is near,
Its steady light dispels all fear,
For hearts aglow, and spirits bright,
Are lifted high on love's sweet flight.

Shadows to Sunshine

From depths of night, where shadows sway,
A ray of hope begins its play,
It dances bright, through gloom it weaves,
A warming touch that light retrieves.

Out from the dark, the dawn does break,
A promise new in each day's wake,
With beams that kiss the morning dew,
The world is bathed in golden hue.

No shadow stays when light appears,
Though once held close, our darkest fears,
We turn to face the rising sun,
And find the dreams we've just begun.

Let light embrace, and shadows flee,
In sunshine, find our spirits free,
The night a tale from yesteryear,
In daylight's glow, no shadows near.

Breath of Fresh Air

A gentle breeze, both cool and light,
Through fields it flows, both day and night,
It whispers tales from far and near,
A breath of life, so pure and clear.

With every gust, our souls revive,
From stagnant holds, they break and thrive,
In open fields, where wildflowers sway,
We find our path, we find our way.

The scent of pine, of ocean's mist,
In nature's hold, we coexist,
With lungs so free, in sky so fair,
We take in deeply, freshened air.

Through winds of change, we boldly go,
A world refreshed, a heart aglow,
In every step, in every stride,
A breath of life, our constant guide.

Small Acts, Big Impacts

A smile can light a stranger's day,
A kind word breaks the darkest gray,
A helping hand in times of strife,
Can change the course of someone's life.

A seed of joy with each good deed,
From simple acts, great love can breed,
A chain of kindness, strong and true,
Begins with actions done by you.

Each gesture, though it may seem small,
Can spread a wealth, uplifting all,
For even tiny sparks can grow,
Into a blaze and brightly glow.

So never doubt the strength you wield,
For love and kindness are your shield,
These small acts, they ripple wide,
Transforming lives on every side.

Remember this as you go forth,
Your heart is boundless in its worth,
Each little step, each choice you make,
Can shift the world with every shake.

A Beacon of Light

Through storms and night, it stands so bright,
A guide to those who've lost their sight,
A steadfast glow, a constant friend,
It shows the way until the end.

In sea of doubt, it pierces through,
A trusted light in skies of blue,
A whisper soft, a gentle call,
To lead us back when we may fall.

When shadows cast their fearful shade,
A beacon's light will never fade,
Its warmth and hope, a growing flame,
In darkest times, it calls our name.

A symbol of unyielding grace,
It shines with love, a warm embrace,
No matter where, or far we roam,
It guides the lost ones safely home.

So be a beacon, strong and true,
Let kindness be the light in you,
For others lost within their night,
Can find their way through your soft light.

Calm amidst Chaos

In swirling winds and tempest's roar,
Find tranquil seas, a peaceful shore,
Within the heart a quiet stream,
A place to wander, rest, and dream.

When life becomes a stormy blast,
Stay anchored firm until it's passed,
Seek out the calm amidst the fray,
And peace will guide you through the day.

The world may rage and skies may fall,
But inner peace can conquer all,
A breath, a pause, a moment's grace,
Can slow the rush, the frantic pace.

Hold tight to stillness, let it grow,
Amidst the chaos, let it show,
The power of a quiet soul,
Can heal, can mend, can make us whole.

So in the tumult, be the calm,
A soothing, gentle, healing balm,
Let chaos come, but know you'll be,
A tranquil island in the sea.

Wisdom from Wounds

The scars we bear, they tell a tale,
Of battles fought, and times we failed,
But in each wound, a lesson learned,
A deeper wisdom has been earned.

Through tears, through pain, we rise anew,
With strength and grace, our spirits grew,
The trials faced, the hardships past,
Have shaped a wisdom built to last.

Each setback was a stepping stone,
To where we've soared, to how we've grown,
And though the pain we've faced was real,
It taught us how to truly heal.

In every mark upon our skin,
A victory, a change within,
For from each tear and every ache,
A wiser soul does gently wake.

So honor wounds and what they preach,
The depths of wisdom they can teach,
For through the scars, we come to know,
The strength, the light, that from us glow.

Guided by Grace

In twilight's glow, we find our way,
Through shadows cast, the light will stay.
A whisper soft, an angel's trace,
Forever led, guided by grace.

Amidst the storms, through dark and drear,
A beacon bright will draw us near.
With gentle hands, our hearts embrace,
We walk this path, guided by grace.

When trials come, our spirits wane,
A grace-filled touch will soothe the pain.
In strength renewed, we lift our face,
Through every storm, guided by grace.

In moments still, when peace is frail,
A quiet calm, a sacred veil.
Through tangled thoughts, a soft solace,
A love divine, guided by grace.

Hand Holding Hope

In tender grip, the warmth we feel,
A silent vow, a bond of steel.
Through doubts and fears, we gently cope,
Together strong, hand holding hope.

In darkest nights, we share the light,
Our dreams alight, shining bright.
With every step, we climb the slope,
United close, hand holding hope.

When shadows fall, our spirits shake,
A gentle squeeze, in love we wake.
Through winding paths, our hearts elope,
A steadfast bond, hand holding hope.

Though distance calls, and time may part,
We'll carry faith within our heart.
With trust and love, no fear will grope,
Forever bound, hand holding hope.

Subtle Embrace

In quiet glades, where whispers sing,
A subtle touch, like dawn in spring.
Unseen but felt, a gentle trace,
The sweetest calm, a subtle embrace.

Through moments hushed, our hearts align,
In fleeting time, a love divine.
With every breath, we find the space,
To hold onto, a subtle embrace.

When silence falls, in twilight's bloom,
A certain peace, dispels the gloom.
With shadows soft, and tender grace,
We find our strength, in subtle embrace.

In echoes faint, where dreams reside,
We feel the bond, a love untried.
Through every storm, in life's brisk chase,
We cherish deep, the subtle embrace.

Beacon of Belief

Through midnight dark, a star will gleam,
A guiding light for every dream.
In faith unwavering, we find relief,
In trials faced, our beacon of belief.

When hopes are lost, and paths unclear,
A glow will shine, to quell our fear.
With courage drawn, our hearts in sheaf,
We journey forth, with beacon of belief.

Through valleys low, and mountains high,
A steadfast light, will never die.
With every doubt, we find our chief,
In steadfast truth, our beacon of belief.

In weary days, when shadows fall,
A radiant glow, will guide us all.
With love as anchor, our soul's motif,
We hold the light, our beacon of belief.

Turning the Tide

When the storm clouds gather overhead,
And waves crash hard against the shore,
We find the strength we thought was dead,
And row our ships to calm once more.

The sea may rage, the wind may howl,
But deep within our spirits rise,
A guiding light, a seafarer's vow,
To brave the storm and clear the skies.

In darkest times, we hold on tight,
Our hands entwined, our hearts aligned,
Together we can face the night,
And turn the tide with love enshrined.

Each trial faced, each challenge met,
We grow in courage, faith, and might,
The sun will rise, we shan't forget,
Through tempest times, we'll find the light.

Roots of Resilience

Beneath the soil, our roots run deep,
Through rock and clay, through time and space,
In trials, our hearts the promise keep,
To rise above with steady grace.

Though winds may bend and storms may break,
Our branches reach for skies anew,
In every fall, a lesson take,
Resilience builds with morning dew.

From seed to tree, our journey long,
Through droughts and floods, through sun and shade,
Each scar a note in nature's song,
Each growth a triumph proudly made.

No gale can fell, no storm can sway,
Our spirits strong, our roots remain,
In life's grand dance, we've found the way,
To bloom once more through joy and pain.

Harbors of Hope

In the stillness of the morning light,
We find a place where dreams reside,
A harbor safe from darkest night,
Where love and hope forever bide.

The lighthouse stands on rocky shores,
Its beacon bright against the storm,
It guides us through the tempest roars,
To safe embrace and hearts that warm.

Within these walls, we reclaim peace,
A sanctuary from the fray,
In harbors where our troubles cease,
We breathe anew, greet each new day.

Anchored firm in the sea of life,
We navigate through joy and strife,
With hope as steady as the wave,
We venture forth, hearts fierce and brave.

Palettes of Positivity

In hues of gold and shades of blue,
We paint our days with vibrant cheer,
A palette bright, a hopeful view,
Each stroke a moment held so dear.

From dawn's first light to twilight's glow,
We find the colors of our soul,
Through highs and lows, our spirits grow,
With every brush, we become whole.

Amidst the gray, a rainbow's arc,
A promise held within the sky,
In every heart, there lies a spark,
A story told in colors high.

With hands held firm and eyes alight,
We craft our world, create our fate,
In palettes filled with pure delight,
We journey forth to dreams so great.

Sunshine on Grey Days

When skies are draped in sullen grey,
And shadows creep through light's decay,
A golden beam breaks through the mist,
With a gentle, warming kiss.

It whispers softly to your soul,
Lifting burdens, making whole,
A silent promise, bright and true,
That sunshine always follows through.

Though clouds may gather, dark and vast,
And storms seem endless as they pass,
Remember always, come what may,
There's sunshine led by hope's array.

In every heart a light will glow,
To chase away the weary woe,
Eclipsing fear with radiant rays,
A beacon on the darkest days.

So hold this truth within your heart,
When shadows grow and dreams depart,
For grey will fade and storm will cease,
And sunshine bring a timeless peace.

A Net Beneath

In moments when you slip and fall,
When hopes and dreams seem very small,
A net beneath will hold you strong,
To cradle you and right the wrong.

Though life may cast you in despair,
With challenges too hard to bear,
There's comfort in the love you keep,
A net beneath your soul to steep.

For woven tight with threads of care,
This safety net is always there,
When trials weigh and burdens toll,
It catches heart and soothes the soul.

In friendships old and new we find,
A net that's crafted, interlined,
With kindness, trust, and faith around,
Its strength within, forever bound.

So trust in love when shadows press,
And lean into its soft caress,
For in this net of boundless grace,
You'll always find a resting place.

Breath to Steady

In throes of chaos, wild and grand,
When life's too much to understand,
A calming breath can steady souls,
And bring the peace that turmoil stole.

Inhale the courage, deep and slow,
Exhale the fear that ebbs and flows,
With every breath, a steady beat,
To guide you through when life's replete.

Amidst the storm's relentless roars,
Find sanctuary in the pores,
Of every breath you take anew,
A rhythm pure, a strength to you.

Let calmness circulate your veins,
Replacing doubt with gentle gains,
For in each breath, a world you mold,
Where every moment turns to gold.

So breathe with purpose, deep and true,
For breath can cleanse and life renew,
Inhaled with hope, exhaled with grace,
A steady heart in every space.

Unseen Guardians

Beyond the veil where shadows drift,
Unseen guardians gently lift,
With silent wings and watchful eyes,
They guard us from the hidden cries.

In whispers soft and touch unseen,
They mend the spaces in-between,
Eclipsing doubt with tender might,
Embracing us in darkest night.

A presence felt, though seldom known,
In moments when we feel alone,
Their gentle guidance steers us clear,
Through treacherous paths, they conquer fear.

Unseen by eyes yet always there,
They blanket us in boundless care,
For every trial, every tear,
Their unseen strength will draw us near.

So trust the guardians in the air,
For they are with you, everywhere,
With unseen hands and loving grace,
They guard each step that you embrace.

Threads of Trust

In whispers soft, the heart will weave,
A tapestry of dreams believed.
Though time will tug, and shadows thrust,
We find our strength in threads of trust.

A gentle hand, a whispered vow,
The stars above bear witness now.
Through storms that bend and tempests gust,
We stitch anew our threads of trust.

In eyes that meet, a silent pledge,
A bond that none could e'er allege.
Though life may fray, we turn the rust,
To shining gold, our threads of trust.

By candlelight, in night's embrace,
We trace the lines of love and grace.
For in the dark, when paths are just,
We hold onto our threads of trust.

With ages past and futures vast,
In every moment, truth is cast.
The fabric strong, from dusk to dust,
Is woven deep with threads of trust.

Holding On

Beneath a sky both bold and blue,
In quiet moments, thoughts accrue.
We find our hearts, a common song,
In waves of time, we're holding on.

The hands of fate, they push and pull,
Through seasons bright and moments dull.
In love's embrace where we belong,
The strength we find in holding on.

When shadows pale and courage weak,
In whispered prayer, our spirits speak.
The night may stretch, however long,
We'll see it through by holding on.

Through laughter bright and bitter tears,
In joy and pain throughout the years.
Together we will right the wrong,
By faith alone, we're holding on.

Though time may age and faces change,
Our hearts remain within the same.
In every note, a lasting song,
Forevermore, we're holding on.

Quiet Counsel

In silence deep, where wisdom lives,
A gentle touch, the dark forgives.
A guiding light, a mentor's spell,
We find our truth in quiet counsel.

Through whispered words, a path we find,
A melding of both heart and mind.
When doubts arise and fears compel,
We're soothed anew by quiet counsel.

With every breath, the soul renews,
In tranquil calm, we find our muse.
The world may roar, yet faith will swell,
Within the grace of quiet counsel.

In moments hushed, where shadows weigh,
A beacon shines to light the way.
From storm's embrace, we bid farewell,
And trust the course of quiet counsel.

In hearts attuned, in minds unchained,
The essence of the truth is gained.
Through life's terrain, we will propel,
Guided always by quiet counsel.

Calm Currents

On rivers wide where waters flow,
In tranquil grace, we learn to grow.
Through life's embrace and moments swift,
We journey on calm currents' drift.

The tides may turn, the winds may shift,
Yet peace abides in gentle lift.
A voyage true, our spirits swift,
We sail along calm currents' drift.

In moonlit waves, reflections dance,
A timeless waltz in love's expanse.
Through stormy nights and daylight's gift,
We find our way, calm currents' drift.

With every bend, a lesson learned,
In stillness deep, our hearts are turned.
The waters smooth, our souls uplift,
In silent song, calm currents' drift.

Through ebb and flow, we're carried forth,
In steadfast bond, we know our worth.
From dawn till dusk, we always drift,
In harmony, calm currents' gift.

A Shoulder to Lean On

In times of sorrow, in times of pain,
A shoulder to lean on, through the rain.
When the world feels cold, and burdens weigh,
A friend's embrace keeps fears at bay.

We'll walk together, side by side,
In each other's strength, we will abide.
For in every dawn, and darkest night,
A shoulder to lean on, our guiding light.

Through storms and trials, we'll endure,
With hearts united, firm and sure.
In joy and grief, we'll stand as one,
A shoulder to lean on, till task be done.

Bridges of Understanding

Across the rivers, between our minds,
Bridges of understanding, our souls confined.
With open hearts and hands extended,
We find the peace where love's intended.

In shared stories and tender smiles,
We bridge the gaps across the miles.
Differences fade, and spirits blend,
On bridges of understanding, we mend.

Through words of hope and acts of grace,
We build a world, a kinder place.
No longer strangers, hearts of kin,
On bridges of understanding, we begin.

Embrace of Warmth

In the chill of night, in winter's breath,
An embrace of warmth defies death.
Soft whispers of comfort, arms entwined,
In each other's love, solace we find.

Fires may fade, but hearts remain,
In the embrace of warmth, free from pain.
Through the darkest cold, we boldly go,
With love's pure heat, we brightly glow.

In tender moments, trust be thine,
An embrace of warmth, souls align.
In kindness shared, we overcome,
Hand in hand, a new day begun.

Steps Toward Healing

With wounded hearts, we slowly tread,
Steps toward healing, where we're led.
Past the shadows, into the light,
Each step forward, a victory in sight.

In whispered prayers and solemn vows,
We seek the peace the heart allows.
Through every trial, and tear once shed,
Steps toward healing, by love we're fed.

Hand in hand, we'll find our way,
With courage born of each new day.
Every trial faced, each fear revealed,
Are steps toward healing, and wounds healed.

Shimmer of Support

In hands that lift when shadows fall,
A gentle touch, a whispered call,
Through woven bonds of unseen art,
Lies the shimmer of support.

When teardrops meet the sliding rain,
Or quiet echoes mix with pain,
A shoulder, strong, amidst the night,
Brings a shimmer into sight.

With every smile we bravely share,
A reassurance, soft as air,
In darkened rooms where fears distort,
Flickers a shimmer of support.

United under skies of grey,
Two hearts may guide each other's way,
Through every storm and tempest wrought,
There sparkles a shimmer, dearly sought.

And though the path is steep and long,
Together we are twice as strong,
In unity our spirits sort,
And find the shimmer of support.

Compass to Calm

In tumult's grip, with restless heart,
The world a maze, each turn an art,
Seek within, a stillness draught,
Find the compass to your calm.

Amidst the chaos, breathe in slow,
Let tranquil waters gently flow,
Through inner peace, your chart drawn neat,
Follow the compass, its truth sweet.

When life's gales begin to roar,
A quiet harbor at your core,
Anchor there, let go of qualm,
And steer by the compass to calm.

In twilight's hush or dawn's first light,
An inner guide, both day and night,
Navigates through strife's alarm,
Trust the compass to your calm.

With every step, through every plight,
A gentle presence, strong as might,
Guides the way, a soothing psalm,
Through life's compass, find your calm.

Threading the Dark

When shadows stretch and stars retreat,
And silence sings its coldest beat,
A slender thread through night's remark,
Begins the art of threading dark.

In whispered winds that breach the still,
Through ghostly fogs and twilight's chill,
One thread to pull, a hopeful spark,
Grants courage for threading dark.

The moon's faint glow, a guiding lamp,
Amidst the night's oppressive ramp,
Soft hands weave tales of ancient lark,
Their wisdom in threading dark.

With heart alight, through realms unknown,
Where fears have carved their silent throne,
One dares to mend each fragile mark,
While bravely threading through the dark.

At dawn's first blush, the thread's complete,
A tapestry of light and feat,
Each woven strand, a brave embark,
On the journey of threading dark.

Gentle Persistence

Like rain that carves through valiant stone,
With drops that fall, but not alone,
Through time and trial, its path insists,
A tale of gentle persistence.

When mountains rise, imposing, tall,
Small steps, though faint, can conquer all,
With grace and strength their course subsist,
The mark of gentle persistence.

In lives where dreams may seem too far,
A steady hand can raise a star,
No storm can cease what love insists,
When held with gentle persistence.

Through harshest days or nights of cold,
A steadfast heart breaks every mold,
Each forward reach, an act of gist,
Embodies gentle persistence.

With every dawn, a fresh pursuit,
In patient grounds, the seeds take root,
Through trials, time, we shall insist,
To thrive in gentle persistence.

Guiding Light in the Gloom

In shadowed depths of sorrow's night,
A glow emerges, ever bright.
Through darkest paths, it leads the way,
Turning night into day.

When hope seems lost, and hearts grow weak,
This light is ours, and not so bleak.
It whispers soft, our fears dispel,
In its warmth, we dwell.

It shines in corners, far and near,
Dispelling shadows, quelling fear.
Guiding steps with gentle grace,
A beacon in this place.

With every dawn, it rises strong,
A promise kept, where we belong.
Through every trial, storm, or fright,
It remains, our guiding light.

Whispers of Reassurance

In quiet moments, soft and clear,
A whisper comes, dissolving fear.
Words of comfort, gently spoken,
Mending hearts that once were broken.

When dreams fade into the night,
Whispers turn them back to light.
In every sigh and silent plea,
Comfort finds a way to be.

Through life's trials, fierce and tough,
Whispers say, "You are enough."
In the stillness, they surround,
Lifting spirits from the ground.

With every echoed, soothing tone,
You are never quite alone.
Whispers of reassurance, dear,
Always tender, always near.

Beacon Through the Storm

Amidst the tempest, wild and free,
A beacon shines for all to see.
Through winds that howl and seas that rage,
It stands unyielding, age to age.

Its light, a promise, strong and true,
Guides vessels lost, and hearts anew.
Through storm and night, it holds its ground,
A steadfast glow, so profound.

When all seems lost in swirling tides,
This beacon's light in darkness hides.
Yet still it shines, a guiding mark,
Illuminating through the dark.

With every wave, each thunder's roar,
It calls us safely to the shore.
Beacon through the storm, our guide,
In its glow, we do reside.

Soothe the Ache

In times of sorrow, hearts that break,
A gentle touch can soothe the ache.
Soft words of love, a tender embrace,
Bring comfort in the hardest place.

When tears flow freely, eyes grown dim,
A whisper speaks of hope within.
A hand to hold, and time to heal,
These moments shared, the heart can feel.

Through pain that lingers, shadows cast,
The promise comes, this too shall pass.
Healing comes with each new dawn,
In strength renewed, we carry on.

With solace found in bonds we keep,
In quiet hours when shadows creep.
Soothe the ache, and mend the soul,
Love's tender touch makes us whole.

Embrace of Understanding

In twilight hues, we find our peace,
Among the whispers of the breeze,
Together, hearts begin to ease,
As doubts and fears, they find release.

In moonlit nights, truths softly gleam,
Illuminating every dream,
In unity, we stitch the seam,
Of moments lost, now flowing stream.

Each thought entwined, a tender bind,
Compassion flowing, intertwined,
With gentle grace, we heal the mind,
And leave the harsh regrets behind.

In silent glances, stories weave,
A tapestry where hearts believe,
Despite the pain, we shall achieve,
The strength to grow, to interleave.

Together, we will write the tale,
Of love that stands, though trials assail,
In every breath, our souls exhale,
The warmth of understanding's veil.

Hands to Steady

When storms arise, and skies turn gray,
In shadows cast, I'll find my way,
With hands to steady, come what may,
Together, in this dance we'll stay.

Through turbulent, uncharted seas,
We'll navigate with gentle ease,
With courage stitched in every breeze,
Our hearts aligned, like guardian trees.

Amid the trials, fierce and vast,
In moments where the future's cast,
I'll hold you close until the last,
And steady you as shadows pass.

In trust and faith, our spirits shine,
Each heartbeat echoes through the line,
With steady hands, your strength is mine,
In harmony, our souls align.

Together, we shall brave the night,
With steadfast grip, and courage bright,
Through every tempest, darkest plight,
Our hands will steady, hearts take flight.

Between the Shadows

Between the shadows, light will play,
A dance of dusk, the end of day,
In twilight's hold, where dreams convey,
A whispered hope that finds its way.

In silken threads, the night is spun,
As stars align with moon and sun,
In hidden realms, our hearts become,
A tapestry of worlds begun.

With every breath, a fleeting chance,
To waltz within this shadowed trance,
In delicate, entwined romance,
Where darkness meets the daylight's glance.

Beyond the realms of sight and sound,
In spaces where the lost are found,
We'll wander through, and there be crowned,
By memories in nightfall bound.

Between the shadows, we will seek,
The voice of night, so soft and meek,
In whispered tones, our hearts will speak,
Of love and dreams both bold and sleek.

Searching for Solace

Through winding paths and meadows wide,
In search of solace, hearts abide,
With gentle steps, our fears we hide,
And follow where the dreams reside.

In morning's light, a promise new,
With every dawn, a brighter hue,
In quiet moments we pursue,
A solace in the skies' soft blue.

Amidst the world's relentless pace,
We find a haven, find our place,
In tender arms, a sweet embrace,
Where solace graces every space.

With whispered winds, the trees will sigh,
As time and troubles drift and fly,
In solace found, our spirits rise,
A calm beneath the azure sky.

Together, we will journey far,
Beneath the moon, a guiding star,
In search of solace, near and far,
We'll find the peace of who we are.

Glowing Reassurance

In twilight's gentle, calming hue,
A beacon's light begins to show,
Through shadows cast, the night's eschew,
A whispered promise softly glows.

Beneath the sky of endless stars,
A cradle for the weary heart,
Through endless time and countless scars,
A sacred pledge we'll never part.

In candles' flames and hearth's embrace,
The world dissolves, the fears subside,
In silent nights, our fears we face,
Together here, no need to hide.

The gentle hand, the loving glance,
In darkness, light will always bloom,
A steadfast trust, an endless chance,
To banish every shade of gloom.

Beyond the night, the dawn will rise,
In every heart, a light renewed,
With glowing warmth to claim the skies,
Reassured by love imbued.

Bridge over Troubled Waters

When tempests rage and torrents pour,
A bridge stands strong, steadfast and sure,
A pathway through the storm's uproar,
Where hope persists, serene and pure.

Beneath the arch, the waters churn,
Yet steps are placed with careful grace,
A journey toward safe return,
From chaos to a peaceful place.

The planks may creak, the anchors strain,
Yet bonds endure, the ties hold fast,
A traveler endures the pain,
For solace found at journey's last.

Clouds shall part, the skies will clear,
The bridge remains through night and day,
To cross it is to cast out fear,
A guiding light along the way.

O'er troubled waters, calm shall be,
For every heart that dares to tread,
A bridge to span eternity,
With hope and love to forge ahead.

Softened Edges

In mornings soft with pastel light,
The world awakens, edges blurred,
As shadows yield to gentle might,
A symphony of whispered word.

The harshest lines begin to fade,
In tender hues of dawn's embrace,
The soul finds solace, unafraid,
In moments clasped, a sacred place.

Where once the world was sharp and keen,
Now soft with love's unfaltering flow,
A landscape robed in tranquil sheen,
Where whispered winds through meadows blow.

Upon each crest, a velvet kiss,
Of sunlight dancing, tenderly,
To shape the day with boundless bliss,
And soften life's complexity.

In softened edges lies the key,
A truth revealed as day unfolds,
That love can blur the lines we see,
And gently shape what future holds.

Resonance of Care

In whispered tones and soft caress,
The resonance of care is found,
Through quiet moments, love professed,
In silence, joy and peace abound.

A hand to hold, a gentle smile,
In every act of kindness shown,
Through distance, yet with every mile,
The seeds of care are deeply sown.

No words required, the heart will speak,
In deeds that render love so clear,
A melody both strong and meek,
Resonance felt when one is near.

In laughter shared and tears embraced,
The bonds of care will only grow,
An endless source of purest grace,
In hearts where true compassion flows.

Through storm and sun, in loss or gain,
This resonance remains the same,
A testament to love's refrain,
The glorious sound of care proclaimed.

A Light to Navigate

Through tempest and drought, we find our way,
A lantern's glow, at night and day,
Guiding hearts both lost and true,
A beacon bright in shades of blue.

When darkness grips and hope seems slight,
It pierces through, a radiant light,
Each step we take, with fear allayed,
In gentle beams, our doubts are swayed.

Oft we lose the path we've known,
Yet in its warmth, no heart's alone,
For even in the shadows deep,
It calls us forth from endless sleep.

With every storm and raging sea,
Its glow ensures we'll always see,
A brighter day that lies ahead,
Where dreams reside and fears have fled.

A light to navigate, steadfast and strong,
Guiding through the right and wrong,
In every heart, its flame persists,
A guiding star that still insists.

Compassionate Echoes

In quiet whispers, hearts do speak,
In tender moments, soft and meek,
A resonance that gently grows,
A chorus sweet, compassion flows.

In times of trial, hands extend,
With warmth and care, they make amends,
A kindness shared, a smile returned,
A lesson deep in love is learned.

Echoes ring through silent tears,
Banishing our hidden fears,
A voice of solace in the night,
A beacon in our darkest plight.

Each act of grace, a ripple starts,
A healing balm for broken hearts,
With every word and deed that's shown,
A thread of comfort, deeply sewn.

Oh, compassionate echoes, wise and true,
You weave a bond 'tween me and you,
A symphony of love's refrain,
Eternal, ever to remain.

Comfort in the Chaos

When life unravels at the seams,
And nightmares drown our sweetest dreams,
Within the storm, a tranquil place,
Where peace reveals her gentle face.

Amidst the clamor, chaos reigns,
Yet in the stillness, calm maintains,
A sanctuary, unseen, discreet,
A refuge from the frenzy's beat.

Fleeting time, a swift cascade,
Through it all, foundations laid,
In chaos, strength, we come to find,
A quietude of heart and mind.

Every moment, pure and clear,
A space where we can shed our fear,
Finding solace, deep within,
Where true serenity begins.

Comfort in the chaos, deep,
A promise made our souls to keep,
Through tumult, trials, life's cruel jest,
In peace, we find our needed rest.

Shelter in Words

In lines and stanzas, refuge found,
A world of quiet, safe and sound,
Where letters form a sacred space,
A haven bright with endless grace.

Each verse a shield from bitter cold,
In whispered prose, a truth is told,
A tapestry of thought unfurled,
A shelter in a noisy world.

The weight of words, both soft and strong,
In verse and rhyme, we find our song,
A melody of hope and light,
To guide us through the darkest night.

For in this script, our hearts align,
In every phrase, a star doth shine,
A constellations' gentle glow,
In words, the path is sure to show.

Shelter in words, a home so dear,
Residing close, drawing near,
A poet's soul within us teems,
In written lines, we're free to dream.

Whispers of Comfort

In the hush of twilight, soft voices call,
Whispers of comfort, in the evening's fall.
Gentle as moonlight, they wrap us warm,
Shielding the heart from impending storm.

Breezes of solace, in lullabies sweet,
Cradle the weary, souls gently meet.
The night sings a hymn, serene and true,
Whispers of comfort in skies painted blue.

The leaves tell a story in rustling sound,
Of peace ever-present, always around.
Echoes of laughter, memories dear,
Whispers of comfort in moments so clear.

Embrace the quiet, let your heart mend,
In whispers of comfort, the soul will ascend.
Journey through shadows with courage in hand,
In whispers of comfort, together we stand.

The dawn will break soft, with light anew,
Whispers of comfort, like morning dew.
Hold to the silence, let it enfold,
In whispers of comfort, find stories untold.

Strength to Lean On

In times of turmoil, when storms rage high,
Strength to lean on, beneath the wide sky.
Hands that steady, hearts that renew,
Find strength to lean on in days we go through.

Shoulders to cry on, and words to uplift,
Strength in the bonds that heal every rift.
Faith in each other, a fortress of trust,
Strength to lean on when the world turns to dust.

Eyes that are watchful, guarding the heart,
Strength to lean on when worlds fall apart.
In the quietest moments, the hardest of cries,
Strength to lean on in someone's gentle eyes.

Paths we have traveled with friends by our side,
Strength to lean on in life's ebb and tide.
Through valleys of shadow, through peaks of light,
Strength to lean on both day and night.

In the arms of compassion, let love be the guide,
Strength to lean on, with nothing to hide.
Embrace every challenge, face every fear,
Find strength to lean on with someone near.

Echoes of Empathy

In the depths of our hearts, soft whispers reside,
Echoes of empathy, where kindness won't hide.
In silence and shadow, we find the true songs,
Of echoes of empathy, where each spirit belongs.

Tales of the weary, in eyes softly told,
Echoes of empathy in gestures unfold.
We carry each burden, as if it were ours,
Echoes of empathy in life's fleeting hours.

Through valleys of sorrow, where tears gently fall,
Echoes of empathy answer the call.
In laughter and joy, in struggles we know,
Echoes of empathy in hearts everglow.

The strength in our hands when another's needs grow,
Echoes of empathy in actions we show.
Compassion unbridled, love's infinite grace,
Echoes of empathy in every embrace.

With courage, let's walk where fear used to bind,
Echoes of empathy in hearts intertwined.
In unity's power, may we always see,
Echoes of empathy, setting souls free.

A Gentle Push Forward

When twilight whispers dreams to ears,
In shadows' cradle, doubts may sleep.
With dawn's first light, a path appears,
A gentle push, your soul to keep.

Mountains tall and valleys deep,
Each step you take through doubts unwind.
In every stumble, strength you'll reap,
With hope and courage well entwined.

Whispers from the past may rise,
To test the heart with shadows cast.
Yet in your eyes, the future lies,
A gentle push, fears fade at last.

The winds of change may howl severe,
And challenge every steadfast stand.
But with each forward step held dear,
A gentle push, you'll take command.

So let your spirit's banner rise,
Embrace the day with hopeful cheer.
With every dawn, a new surprise,
A gentle push, to persevere.

Light in Dark Times

When skies seem weary, heavy gray,
And shadows dance with haunting grace,
Remember this: there comes a day,
When light will brighten every space.

In darkest hours, dreams falter,
Doubts may grip with silent cries.
Yet in your heart, that flame won't alter,
A steadfast beacon in your eyes.

Through storms and trials, true colors gleam,
Resilience shines, both soft and bright.
In every challenge, find the theme,
Of strength that rises with the night.

For even in the deepest dark,
A glimmer grows, pure and warm.
Hold tight that tiny, glowing spark,
And face the tempest, calm in storm.

So trust in light, no matter small,
For it will guide through realms unknown.
In darkest times, it answers all,
A guiding star in nightwind blown.

Echoes of Reassurance

In the heart of quiet night,
Soft whispers float, like summer breeze.
They carry with them gentle light,
Calming souls with endless ease.

Though doubts may knock upon your door,
And fears may find their way inside,
Echoes of reassurance soar,
Through halls where shadows long reside.

In every tear, there's strength concealed,
In every sigh, a breath reborn.
These echoes calm, they gently yield,
A sense of peace from night till morn.

Amidst the clamor, find your peace,
Within the echoes' soothing song.
In moments still, let worries cease,
And know that you, dear heart, belong.

For every whisper shares a truth,
That in your core, resilience thrives.
These echoes of your dreams, in sooth,
Will guide you, while your spirit strives.

Wings of Encouragement

When life's demands grow heavy, stern,
And shoulders feel the weight of care,
Know that with each twist and turn,
Wings of hope will lift you there.

Through storms of doubt and fearsome gale,
Your inner strength will rise and soar.
In every setback, choose to prevail,
With wings of courage at your core.

No mountain high, no valley low,
Can tether dreams or cage your heart.
On wings of faith, watch as you grow,
And play your destined, wondrous part.

For in your spirit, boundless grace,
And in your soul, a fire burns bright.
With wings of love, find your own pace,
And navigate through darkest night.

So trust those wings that softly span,
And guide you to your sure ascent.
For you possess the master plan,
On wings of encouragement.